POSITIVE STEPS

Dealing with differences

Susan Martineau

with illustrations by Hel James

W
FRANKLIN WATTS
LONDON • SYDNEY

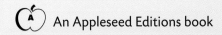 An Appleseed Editions book

First published in 2011 by Franklin Watts
338 Euston Road, London NW1 3BH

Franklin Watts Australia
Hachette Children's Books
Level 17/207 Kent St, Sydney, NSW 2000

© 2011 Appleseed Editions

Created by Appleseed Editions Ltd,
Well House, Friars Hill, Guestling,
East Sussex TN35 4ET

Designed and illustrated by Hel James
Edited by Mary-Jane Wilkins
Picture research by Su Alexander

ISBN 978-1-4451-0363-1

Dewey Classification: 155.2'4

A CIP catalogue for this book is available from the British Library.

Picture credits
Contents page Dick Luria/Thinkstock; 4t Stockbyte/Thinkstock, b BananaStock/Thinkstock; 5 Stockbyte/
Thinkstock; 6 AraBus/Shutterstock; 8 Phase4Photography/Shutterstock; 9,10, 11, 12, 13 & 14t Thinkstock,
b Jupiterimages/Thinkstock; 15 BananaStock/Thinkstock; 16t & br Thinkstock, bl Jack Hollingsworth/
Thinkstock; 17t Hemera Technologies/Thinkstock, b Thinkstock; 18 Jupiterimages/Thinkstock;
19 Rohit Seth/Shutterstock; 20 Shutterstock; 21 Creatas Images/Thinkstock; 22 Digital Vision/Thinkstock;
23 Pixland/Thinkstock; 24 Jupiterimages/Thinkstock; 25t Benis Arapovic/Shutterstock, b Jupiterimages/
Thinkstock; 26 Jupiterimages/Thinkstock; 26-27 background Thinkstock; 27 Jack Hollingsworth/Thinkstock;
28-29 Lakov Kalinin/Shutterstock; 32 Darrin Klimek/Thinkstock
Front cover Mamahoohooba/Shutterstock

Printed in Singapore

Franklin Watts is a division of Hachette Children's Books,
an Hachette UK company.
www.hachette.co.uk

Contents

Everyone is different   4

Don't judge too soon   6

Be yourself!   8

Football for everyone   10

Dealing with racism   12

Understanding each other   14

What do you believe?   16

Try something different   18

I can do that!   20

Respecting older people   22

Welcoming new people   24

Friends across the world   26

Celebrating differences   28

Words to know   30

Index   32

It's fun to meet different people.

Everyone is different

Everyone is different. Imagine how boring it would be if we were all the same. Our differences make the world a wonderful, exciting place.

Our differences do not mean that some people are better than others. We are all just as important as each other, and we should feel proud of the way we are.

LET'S TALK ABOUT...

Think of all the ways people can be different. See if you can add more words to the list below. It might take a long time!

short

tall

old

dark-haired

young

fair-haired

Don't judge too soon

Sometimes we might decide whether we like someone or not from their appearance, or the way they look. We cannot really know someone just by looking at them.

We are judging too soon if we think someone is not nice just because they look a bit different from us, or if they behave in a different way. This is called being prejudiced.

Think about the ways you and your friends are different from each other. Some differences are small and some are large. None of these differences stops you from being friends with each other.

The favourites game

Sit next to someone you do not normally sit with. Look at the person and, without speaking to them, write down three things about them:

- their favourite food
- their favourite TV programme
- their favourite colour

Now ask them and see if you are right about them!

My favourite colour is red.

Does he like blue or red best?

Be yourself!

Rhiannon likes to be with her friends but sometimes she does not really like the things they say about other people.

Rhiannon feels bad because she does not really agree with the others. She does not want to say what she thinks because she does not want to lose her friends.

LET'S TALK ABOUT...

Do you think it would be better if Rhiannon just said what she thought? Can you think of times when you have said or done things because you did not want to seem different from your friends? It is not always easy to speak up for yourself.

I like maths!

I prefer English!

What can you do?

- Decide what you like and dislike for yourself.

- Have confidence in what you think and believe is right.

- Don't just follow the crowd.

- Remember that there is nothing wrong with being different.

- Be yourself!

I don't really like this TV programme they all love.

9

Football for everyone

Alice and Amber have always loved playing football, but the boys at school won't let them play because they are girls. Even the other girls think they should be playing different games with them instead.

Boys and girls are different, but they should be given the same, or equal, chance to do things. When someone is not allowed to do something because they are a girl or a boy this is a kind of prejudice called sex discrimination.

Girls are useless at football! You can't play.

Ballet and dance are great fun for both boys and girls.

LET'S TALK ABOUT...

Can you think of other ways that girls or boys are sometimes treated differently? What do you think of this?

Let us have a go and we can show you how good we are!

Word power

Get into pairs and talk about how you might persuade the boys to let Amber and Alice play football. Think of what you might say.

Dealing with racism

Charlie has made friends with a new boy called Jamal, but some of the other children are saying horrible things about him. Charlie is writing to his friend Ben about it.

When someone is teased or bullied because they come from a different country, or their skin is a different colour, this is called racism. Racism is a kind of discrimination. We should remember that the important thing is the kind of person someone is. It does not matter where they come from or what they look like.

Hi Ben

I hope you are having fun in your new school. There is a new boy here called Jamal. I like him but some of the others say horrible things about him because he has dark skin. They're mean.

See you soon.

Charlie

• A race is a group of people who come from the same part of the world and have the same colour skin and type of hair.

• A racist is someone who treats other people unfairly because they belong to a different race.

• Racism is against the law.

What can you do?

• Tell anyone who makes racist remarks that it is wrong.

• Don't laugh when someone makes racist jokes.

• Don't pass on racist jokes.

• Comfort anyone you see being bullied like this.

• Tell a grown-up you trust if the racist bullying does not stop or you are bullied in this way.

Understanding each other

There are many different countries and races of people in our fascinating world. People speak many different languages. Some people can speak more than one language.

I speak Urdu.

I speak Spanish.

When people leave their own country to live somewhere else they bring their language with them as well as their different customs, or ways of doing things. We can learn a lot about the world by getting to know them.

I speak Chinese and English.

What can you do?

● Be welcoming to people from other countries.

● If they cannot speak your language you can help them to learn.

● Learn some of their language too!

Reading stories is a good way to learn a language.

un   ek

yí   uno

1   one

Language challenge!

You or your friends may come from another country. The children in your class may know lots of different languages. Find out how many languages you know altogether. Then see if you can learn how to count to ten in each one. You could even learn a song in a different language too.

deux   do

èr   dos

2   two

3   teen   tres

trois   sān   three

15

What do you believe?

There are many different religions in the world. A religion is what people believe about God or gods and how they pray or worship.

We should respect the beliefs and religions of other people. They should also respect ours. It is fun to find out about other people's religions and their festivals or celebrations. Sometimes people wear different clothes or eat different food because of their religion.

Muslims pray five times a day.

Christians believe in one God and his son Jesus Christ.

Hindus believe in many gods.

Can you think of some different religions? Look below for some ideas. What religions do you and your friends follow? Not everyone follows a religion.

I'm not sure what I believe yet.

Christianity

Christmas

Time to celebrate

Choose a religious festival or celebration. Here are some ideas to get you started but there are many, many others to discover. Find out about the story behind the festival and how it is celebrated.

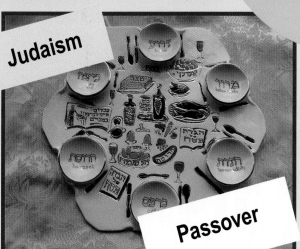

Judaism

Passover

Diwali

Hinduism

Try something different

People around the world eat all kinds of different and delicious food. Perhaps you have a friend from another country where the food is different from yours.

Sometimes people eat certain food because of their religion or what they believe. They might be vegetarian. This means they do not eat meat. Some people eat with knives and forks and others use chopsticks or their hands.

Sook Ling eats noodles with chopsticks.

Anna's favourite food is fajitas.

Jack enjoys hotdogs.

I love my mum's spicy curries.

LET'S TALK ABOUT...

Ask your friends what their favourite food is. Maybe their family eats different food from yours. If you are invited to eat with them always try the food even if it is not the same as yours.

A world menu

Ask everyone in your class to name a dish from another country. It could be one that they eat at home. Draw a menu of all the different types of dishes.

Our menu

chapattis

spaghetti

pitta bread salad

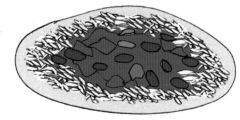

chilli con carne

hamburger

Chinese stir-fried rice

pizza

Thai curry and rice

I can do t

Dan has impaired vision. This is a disability which means he cannot see very well. When he goes out he uses a special stick, called a cane, to help him check where things are.

Dan has lots of other things to help him in class but he knows he can always ask his friends to help too. If someone has a disability this does not mean they cannot join in with everyone else.

Big print on a yellow screen makes it easier to see words on the computer.

My favourite sport is swimming.

Dan's talking watch tells him the time.

LET'S TALK ABOUT...

Can you think of any other disabilities that might make some things difficult to do? Perhaps you have a disability yourself. Remember it is rude to stare or make fun of anyone with a disability.

Where now?

Keep walking straight on.

The guiding game

Put a blindfold on someone who can see. They have to try to find their way from one side of the classroom to the other by feeling their way while the others give directions.

Respecting older people

Sometimes older people seem to have different ways of doing things. We find it hard to imagine that they were once the same age as we are, but old and young people can learn from each other.

Older people have seen and done many things. We can learn lots from listening to them and their stories about life when they were young. We can also help them if they find some things hard to do as they get older.

I'm showing my gran how to use our computer.

My grandpa tells me great stories about when he was young.

What can you do?
- Listen and learn from older people.

- Always be polite and respectful.

- Try and help older people if they are unwell or disabled.

Looking back
Imagine you are 80 years old. Think about some of the amazing inventions of the past 80 years. Then come back to the present and imagine what might be invented during your lifetime.

dishwasher

computers

colour television

mobile phones

Welcoming new people

Aisha and her family had to leave their country because it was too dangerous for them to stay there. She is making friends at her new school but it is hard for her.

Aisha can't speak much English yet.

We're helping her.

LET'S TALK ABOUT...

How do you think Aisha must feel? She has had to leave behind all her old friends and some of her family.

scared

lonely

sad

confused

We like helping Aisha learn English.

What can you do?

- Be welcoming and kind to children like Aisha.

- Never tease them if they cannot understand you.

- Imagine how you would feel if you were Aisha.

My new friends are fun.

Friends across the world

We can learn about different countries and how people live in them by writing letters or emails to a penfriend from another part of the world.

Emails are easy to send, but letters are fun as you see the different stamps from other countries. Always check with a grown-up before emailing or writing to a new friend.

Dear Will

My name is Paulina and I live in Hamburg, Germany. I am learning English at school...

Dear Paulina

Thanks for your letter. Can you tell me more about Germany? What are your hobbies?

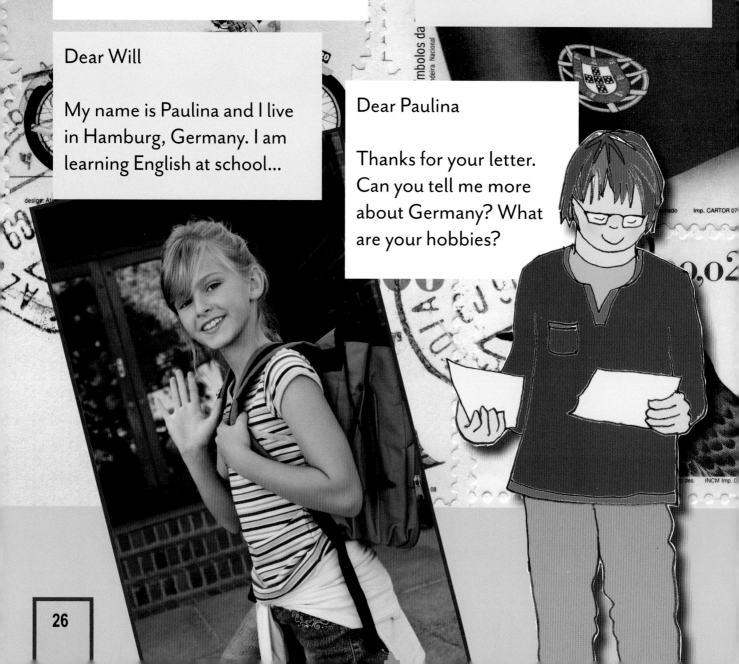

Hi Tyson

What is it like living in New York City? I have only seen it in the movies. Do you play baseball or basketball? I love playing football...

Hi Robbie

I guess my favorite sport is baseball. Do you play that in England?

Getting in touch

Ask your teacher if your class could write to some children in another country. Think of some good questions to ask. Maybe you could have a special board in the classroom to display letters and photos.

Celebrating differences

We can enjoy finding out about people who are different from us. Differences are not something to be afraid of or to dislike. The more we understand about other people, the better we get along with each other.

The important thing about someone is the kind of person they are inside and not what they look like on the outside. We are all equal, no matter where we come from, which language we speak, what clothes we wear or what we believe.

What can you do?
Look at the Words to know on pages 30-31 to make sure you understand what they mean. Make some sentences using them. You could work in pairs and make some drawings to go with them.

All the bold words are explained on pages 30-31.

Be welcoming to people from other countries.

Make a difference – show others you are not prejudiced.

Stick up for what you know is right and be proud to be yourself.

Words to know

appearance
What someone looks like.

belief
What someone believes.

celebrate
To do something special or enjoyable on an important day.

custom
A set way of doing something.

disability
Having a disability means you cannot use a part of your body properly because of illness or an injury.

discrimination
Treating someone unfairly or differently because of their race, sex, religion or disability.

equal
The same as each other.

polite
Having good manners.

prejudiced
Thinking that someone is not equal or the same just because they are different.

race
A group of people who come from the same part of the world and have the same colour skin and type of hair.

racism
Treating people unfairly because they come from a different race.

religion
What people believe about God or gods, and how they pray or worship.

I like getting to know other people.

respect
When you show respect you are careful about the way you treat someone. You show you care about their feelings.

understand
To know about something and what it means.

worship
To show how much you love your God or gods.

Index

beliefs 16, 17, 30
bullying 13

computers 20, 22, 23

dance 11
disabilities 20, 21, 23, 30
discrimination 10, 12, 28, 30

families 24, 25
festivals 16, 17
food 18, 19
football 10, 11, 27
friends 7, 8, 9, 12, 15, 17, 18, 19, 20,
    24, 25, 26, 27

jokes 13

languages 14, 15, 28
likes and dislikes 8, 9
listening 22, 23

older people 22, 23

prejudice 6, 10, 28, 29, 31

racism 12, 13, 31
religion 16, 17, 18, 31

school 12
sex discrimination 10
skin colour 12, 13
sport 20, 27
stories 15, 22, 23
swimming 20

Respect everyone, whoever they are.